My Kind of Music

BOOK 3

Early Intermediate

Kevin Olson

Note from the Composer

Isn't it great when you find a piece of music that perfectly captures who you are, what you like, and how you think? Maybe you really like the title, or the melody stays in your head all day, or maybe it's just simply a blast to play! When you feel that special connection with a musical work, you want to play it and hear it over and over again. I created these compositions with you in mind, hoping that some of them would connect with you in that exciting way. Best wishes in your discovery of pieces about which you could exclaim, "Hey! That's my kind of music!"

Kevin Olson

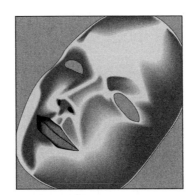

Contents

On the Streets of Cairo

Music from the Middle East has a very distinctive sound. One common characteristic of the music in this region is the lowered second scale degree (in this piece, the A♭). Keep the triple meter graceful by playing the phrases with a light, unaccented touch. Add some light pedal as well, if you wish.

Kevin Olson

6

Sneaking Around

Have you ever tried to tiptoe somewhere, very quietly, so you're not heard? This piece imitates the sound of "sneaking around." Keep your staccato notes light, and your eighth-note patterns unaccented, so you can be as sneaky as possible!

* *Unless otherwise marked, all F's are to be played natural.*

Monument Valley

*In Southern Utah, a few hours from where I grew up, there is one of the most photographed spots
on earth: a desert valley with unusual sandstone formations, mesas, and buttes.
Try to capture the mysterious majesty of Monument Valley by playing the eighth notes lightly and evenly.
Don't forget to bring out the long, lyrical half notes in the melody.*

With wonder ($\quarternote$ = ca. 132)

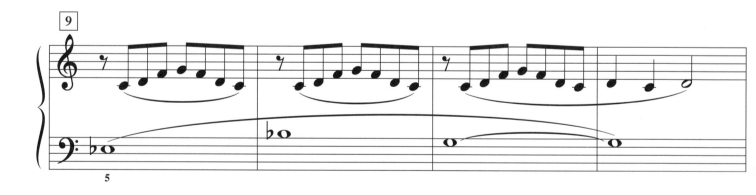

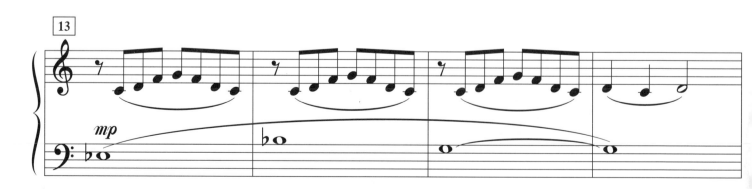

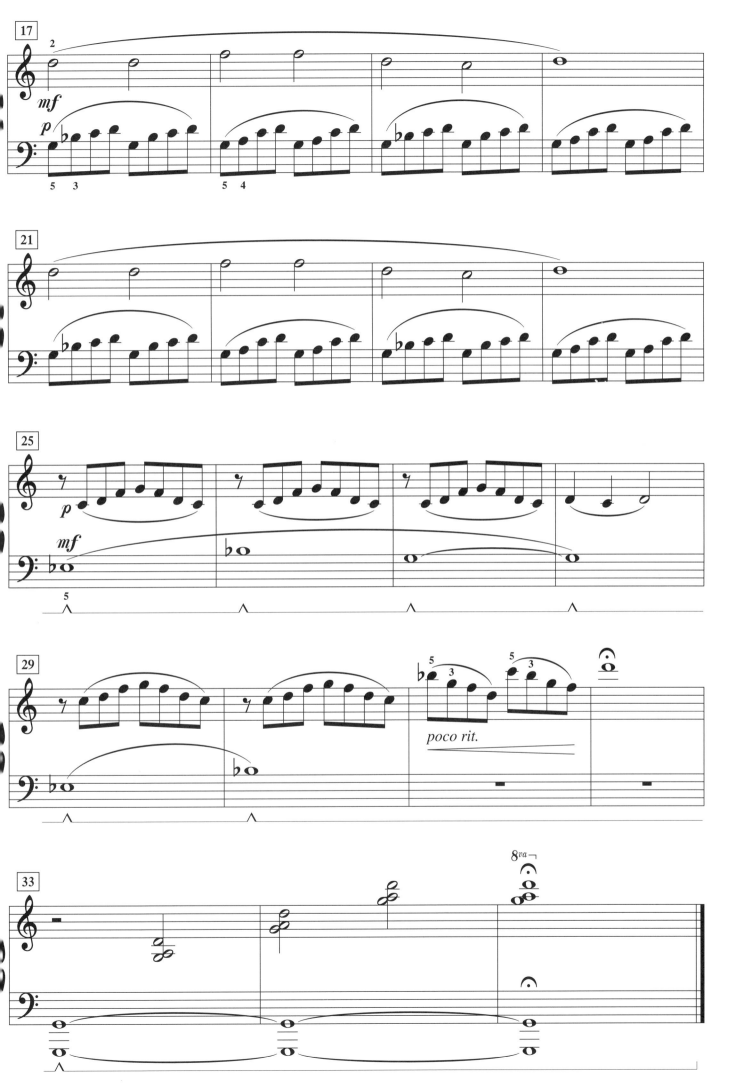

Brave Sea Captain

This sea chanty reflects the courage of sailors who have risked their lives traveling across the ocean.
Sometimes the melody is in the right hand, and sometimes it's in the left.
Make sure you bring out the chanty tune, no matter which hand it's in!

With suspense (♩ = 200 or faster)

Cathedral

Have you ever visited one of those enormous European cathedrals? You walk in and your eyes immediately look to the heavens. This piece captures the awe-inspiring grandeur of the old, Gothic cathedrals by imitating the sound of Gregorian chant. Make this music "breathe" like the chant of many monks by lifting after each phrase and giving each line a direction and shape.

Freely, with majesty; not too quickly ($\quarternote$ = ca. 132)

Masquerade Ball

Picture a fancy ballroom with people dancing while wearing elaborate masks. That is the graceful image this dance portrays. Follow the shape of each melodic phrase and let the dynamics rise and fall as the phrase rises and falls. Don't forget to bring out the left hand in measure 17!

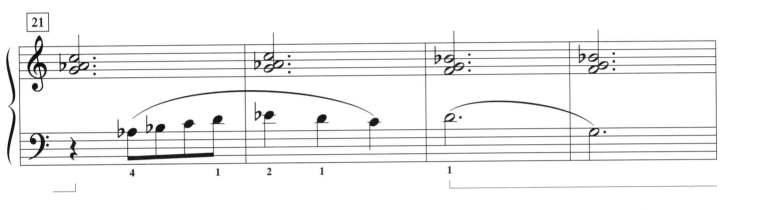

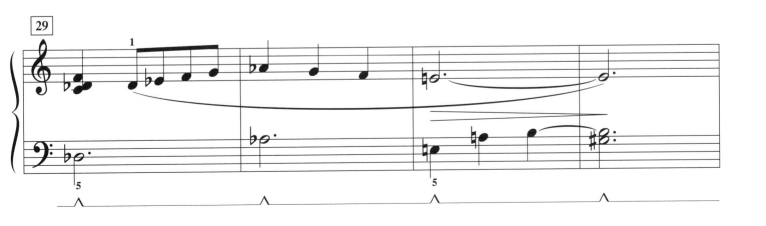

Bad Way to Start the Day

*You know what it's like to wake up on the wrong side of the bed. Everything seems to go wrong, and you haven't
even eaten breakfast yet! This gloomy song recreates the mood of being very grumpy in the morning.
Notice the gradual shifts in dynamics and the pedal changes in each measure.*

In a bad mood (♩ = ca. 120)

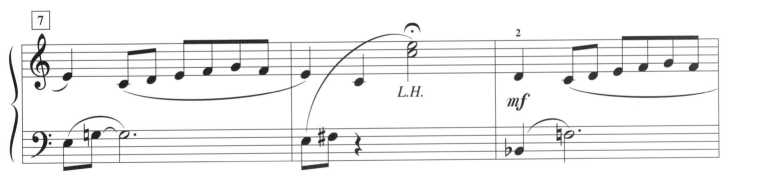

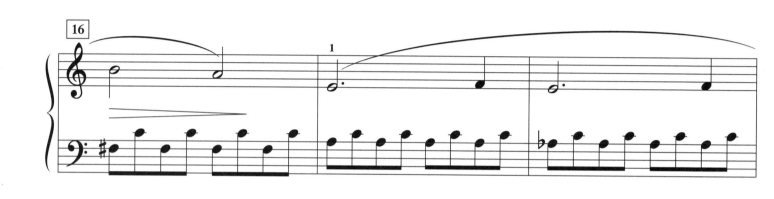

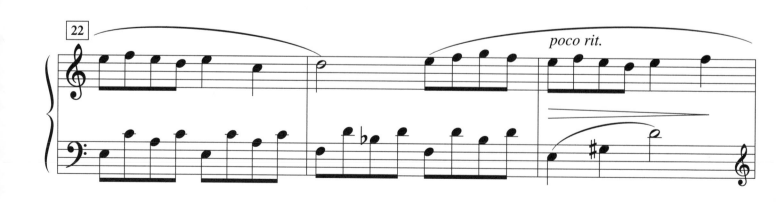

Lazy Afternoon

What a great feeling when you have a whole afternoon with nothing to do! This relaxed feeling can be portrayed in this piece by not playing too quickly, and keeping a legato touch. Put some shape and direction into each phrase to keep things interesting.

Lighthouse in the Storm

*I saw an amazing photograph once that showed a tall white lighthouse in the middle of a raging storm.
A giant wave, almost as tall as the lighthouse, was crashing up against it. This image is reflected in "Lighthouse
in the Storm" through quick, even eighth notes. Keep the tempo steady and the eighth notes light!*

With precision and drama ($\quarternote$ = ca. 200 or faster)

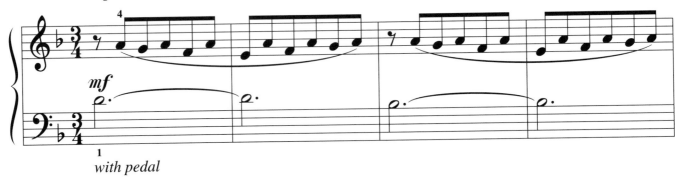